happy

happy

secrets to happiness
from the cultures of the world

MELBOURNE | LONDON | OAKLAND

THE SECRETS

Foreword by Maureen Wheeler, Lonely Planet Co-Founder

HAPPINESS & TRAVEL

There is a story about two children who set out to find a bluebird;
they travel all over the world only to find it in their own backyard.
The bird, of course, represents happiness and the moral of the story
is that happiness is found when you stop looking for it. Travelling
to find happiness is doomed to failure, because happiness comes
in those moments when you are not consciously trying to be happy.
Moments of sheer joy come when you forget yourself and focus
on something other than your own feelings or desires or goals.

When you travel to another country where everything
is unfamiliar, your awareness is heightened, you notice every little
detail because you are trying to make sense of everything going
on around you. The person you are at home becomes less important,
less central to this new story; you are an observer and this sense
of being an outsider intensifies your responses and emotions.

The opportunity to see the world from another viewpoint,
to see yourself as someone foreign, is the adventure of travel.
The freedom, the sense of possibilities, the absence of the mundanity
of normal life, is the excitement of travel. But happiness in travel
comes from the moments when you are aware how lucky you are
to be in that place, at that time, and how wonderful the world is.

INTRODUCTION

Happiness. One word, nine letters, roughly seven billion definitions, one for each person on the planet.

Researchers into emotions and neuroscience say that everyone's level of happiness is about 50% genetically determined, 10% comes from external factors, and the rest comes from how we perceive our circumstances. Money buys us some happiness, they say, but only to the point where we have security – a roof over our heads, a doctor when we're sick, a bit of entertainment.

So why isn't everyone who has reached this level of security perfectly happy? Across the developed world, people have better medical care and longer life spans than ever before. But while many Western countries top the lists of overall happiest countries, many also rank highest in individual rates of depression.

Researchers who study happiness will tell us it's not the flashy car or new shoes that make us happy in the long run. Instead, the most basic aspects of life found in every culture bring us the most joy – connection, mindfulness, gratitude, play. One of the gifts of travel is that it allows us the chance to see how different cultures invite happiness into their lives, whether those countries are rich or poor.

So, does Lonely Planet aim to be the authority on happiness? Heck no. We're still working on it ourselves. We know there are billions of ways to define happiness, but here are 55 we happen to like. They range from physical pleasures like dancing to giving back to your community to accepting the impermanence of life.

The Japanese tea ceremony, and the Ethiopian coffee ceremony remind us to stop and smell the coffee beans and enjoy time spent together. Like *zakat* in Islamic countries or *jimba* in Buddhist lands, the tiny island nation of Tokelau in the South Pacific has a ritual of *inati*, sharing their daily fish catch with those who need it most. In Bhutan the nation defines success not solely by earnings, but by the population's gross national happiness level.

After travelling, your life might change ever so slightly. Maybe after a visit to Italy you take a 15-minute stroll before dinner now and again. Perhaps you invite a friend over for coffee and just talk and laugh for hours, productivity be damned. Or you might start your mornings dancing naked in front of your cat to that calypso music you picked up in the Caribbean. But your eyes are now open and there's no going back, only passing on what you've learned.

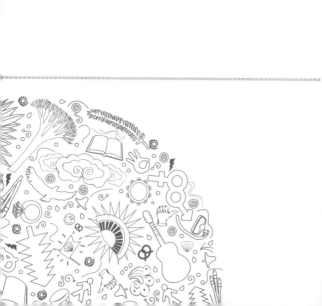

MIND

Secret **Put down in words what you really want**
Tradition **Shinto** *ema* (votive plaques)
Celebrated in **Japan**

If you don't know where you're going, that's where you'll end up

What does happiness mean to you? Good relationships, achievements, material wealth? If you can't define it, you can't achieve it.

Shinto temples in Japan provide small wooden plaques called *ema* for people to write down their desires and hopes. Supplicants might ask for success in exams, a safe journey, a good outcome to a bad situation, or a new car. As each *ema* is completed, it is hung with the others garlanding the temple, for the *kami* (gods) to read.

If the unknowableness of the future feels overwhelming, try writing down a wish list. Think about how you want your life to look. What do you want to achieve? What experiences do you want to have? What kind of person do you want to be? Then put pen to paper.

Expressing your desires in concrete terms helps them seem achievable. It narrows them down to a set of clear goals, landmarks in the map of your future. Then you can start directing your first steps towards the place you want to go.

Secret Prioritise your mental well-being over your financial success
Tradition Gross National Happiness
Celebrated in **Bhutan**

Swap cash for karma

Fast cars, flash houses, laptops, pads, pods and plasma screens. We're all rat-racing to earn money to buy things, to flaunt our wealth and success. But does money make us happy? Global economic growth has risen sharply over the past few decades, but there doesn't appear to have been a commensurate rise in well-being.

What if success could be measured another way? In 1972, King Wangchuck of Bhutan coined the phrase Gross National Happiness. The spiritual well-being of the people, he stated, is more important than the Gross National Product. And Bhutan has maintained its traditions and remains a largely happy place – though those breathtaking mountain views must help.

We may not be able to relocate to the Himalaya, but we can still embrace GNH. Leave work on time to meet friends. Assess whether you're working to live or living to work. And place less emphasis on physical acquisition and more on massaging your mental health.

Secret Let your resentments, worries and sadness go
Tradition *Loy Krathong* (Lantern Festival)
Celebrated in Thailand

Let go of the little things

Sometimes it's the nagging memory of an awkward comment made without thinking. Maybe somone said something to you that stung. You turn the thoughts over till your head gets thick with anxiety.

In northern Thailand, *Loy Krathong* sees thousands of candle-fuelled paper lanterns drift into the night sky, creating an amber glow as these symbols of worry are let go. As they float away, a celebration takes place. Making these little burdens disappear, combined with the beauty of their departure, has a powerful effect.

How can you do this at home? Start with something simple, like writing down each thing that is irritating you on a separate piece of paper. Read each one, give it a moment of consideration, then bin it. Or maybe go outside and let your inner pyromaniac loose, burning each symbol of anxiety, slowly and deliberately. Try practising cloud bursting, assigning each cloud a worry and watching it drift away. Ultimately, it's not how you do it, it's that you do it…

Secret Accept yourself (and others) for who you are
Tradition *La Vela de las Auténticas Intrépidas Buscadoras del Peligro* (Festival of the Authentic, Intrepid Danger-Seekers)
Celebrated in Juchitán, Mexico

Difference is what makes life fabulous

Being different can be rough. Most of us have felt left out or alone. For gay, lesbian and transgender people, this sense of isolation can be acute. Acceptance may be growing but we have a long way to go.

In Juchitán, they're way ahead of the game. The Zapotec people believe in a 'third sex', a category that covers gay and transgender people. Called *muxes* (moo-shays), they're considered a blessing to their families, and are admired for their beauty and talents. At the Zapotec fiesta *La Vela de las Auténticas Intrépidas Buscadoras del Peligro*, *muxes* dress up in colourful Zapotec skirts and hair ribbons to dance, drink and revel in the whole town's attention.

Imagine a world in which everyone was so loved and honoured that they got their own party! Whatever your own personal difference, love yourself for who you are. And if you're not getting that acceptance at home, remember – somewhere out there, someone thinks you're absolutely fabulous.

Secret Have a goal and work towards achieving it
Tradition *Camino de Santiago de Compostela*
(The Way of St James)
Celebrated in **Spain, France and Italy**

Climb every mountain

When was the last time you did something that gave you a real sense of achievement? Our lives can become blurred mosaics of small triumphs and niggling disappointments. We put things off, we let ourselves down, things get lost in the rush.

The *Camino de Santiago de Compostela* is a Catholic pilgrimage with routes stretching from places as far afield as France and Italy, all leading to a church in Spain. It began in medieval times and still attracts flocks of devotees, though for many the meaning has changed. Whatever their reasons, most modern-day pilgrims report having a kind of breakthrough along the way, an epiphany that they never would have achieved without tackling the task.

It may not be possible to take off to Europe right now, but it's always possible to set yourself a challenge. Setting your eyes on that distant mountain and pushing beyond your limits to get there makes you realise just how, well, limiting the very idea of limits can be.

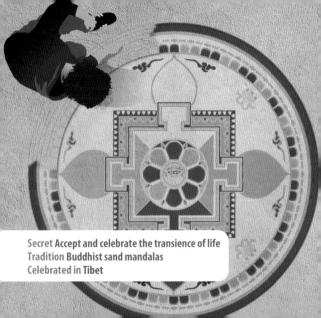

Secret Accept and celebrate the transience of life
Tradition Buddhist sand mandalas
Celebrated in Tibet

Like sand through the hourglass...

Humans have a tendency to put themselves at the centre of the universe. Yet no matter what we do, no matter what we leave behind, time sweeps on: one day we'll all be dust.

Tibetan Buddhists illustrate this inescapable truism by making intricate, brightly glowing mandalas from grains of sand. The sand is poured from metal funnels to make elaborate patterns and the forms of fantastical animals, demons and spiritual symbols.

A mandala can take days or weeks of work to complete, yet when it is finished, the whole creation is swept into an urn. Half the sand is distributed among devotees; the other half is fed to the nearest river, to carry its healing throughout the world.

Celebrating transience is strangely comforting. Draw chalk pictures on your front path, then watch them be worn away by time or rain. Make a sand castle. Accept the inevitable truth that nothing lasts – and savour the peace that comes with it.

Secret Learn to be self-sufficient
in order to feel empowered
Tradition Walkabout
Celebrated in Australia

Get lost to find yourself

In the modern world lifts take you up and down, meals come readymade, and people can be hired to clean your house and mend your car. It's convenient, but it plants a nagging fear: what would I do if none of this existed? Would I be able to cope on my own?

When they reached adolescence, Aboriginal boys would be sent off on walkabout: a lone stroll into the outback for half a year. This rite of passage was deeply connected to the land. Initiates would follow ancient 'songlines', or Dreaming tracks, finding food and shelter from the rocks and trees that sustained their ancestors. They would develop the deep self-awareness that only comes from solitude.

Everyone can take time out. Book a solo holiday – you'll be forced to fend for yourself, and discover what really interests you. Take control of areas in which you feel vulnerable – master basic car mechanics, or learn how to boil an egg. Gain confidence in your own abilities, and take comfort in knowing that you can rely on yourself.

Secret **Forgive – don't let grudges poison you**
Tradition *Paryushan Parva*
Celebrated in **India**

To err is human…

Forgiveness is out of style. Tough guys would rather take an eye for an eye than turn the other cheek. We often forgive only because the alternative is inconvenient or unpalatable. But genuine forgiveness is something else altogether.

Every year, Jains celebrate *Paryushan Parva*. Days of prayer and meditation culminate in a ceremonial asking for and granting of forgiveness. Only in this way, Jains believe, can you truly rid yourself of anger and hostility towards others and cleanse your soul.

To forgive others, you have to have the humility to acknowledge your own imperfections, and forgive yourself. Try writing letters to significant people in your life, apologising for the times you've wounded or failed them (whether you send the letters is up to you). And next time someone wrongs you, why not surprise them by full-heartedly offering them forgiveness – no strings attached. It's amazingly powerful and liberating.

Secret **Put your trust in others and be trusted in return**
Tradition *Castells* (human towers)
Celebrated in Catalonia, Spain

Love – and trust – thy neighbour

It seems we're becoming a less trusting society. It's a sad thing, for a suspicious world is not a happy one.

The tradition of building *castells* (human towers) in Catalonia began in the late 18th century, when the dancers of Valls, near Tarragona, ended jigs by constructing small people-piles. This element of the dance became competitive, and a new sport was born.

The *castell* starts with a *pinya*, a firm base of interlocking bodies. Human tiers are formed by castellers who climb up in a specific order to raise the structure higher, usually between six and 10 levels. The *enxaneta*, the tower's pinnacle, is a lightweight (and brave) child. It's a celebration of a community coming together, putting faith in its fellows to create something unique.

We can't all form human castles but we can forge more open relationships with friends and neighbours, and see other people not as adversaries, but as partners who are vital to our mutual success.

Secret Take a long view rather than expecting instant gratification
Tradition *Tu BiShvat Festival* (New Year for Trees)
Celebrated in Israel

The root less travelled

Technology can give us instant gratification at the click of a button, and we get frustrated when our lives move too slowly. All too often we lose patience and give up when things don't turn out as planned.

In Israel, the Jewish festival of *Tu BiShvat* is celebrated each year with the planting of trees. The festival represents renewal and hope for the future. Children sing songs about the almond tree and eat dates, walnuts and apricots. Aside from nurturing conservation, *Tu BiShvat* shows how nature takes its time. Seeds are planted in winter, then sprout into saplings in spring, but it can be years before the first fruit is enjoyed.

Trees contribute so much to our mental and physical well-being, yet planting one requires discipline, patience and faith. It's a reminder that it's rewarding to delay gratification and see our own efforts bear fruit. Are seeds you planted a long time ago starting to flower? Remember, you also need water, space and time to grow.

Secret **Be grateful for what you have**
Tradition **Thanksgiving**
Celebrated in **USA & Canada**

Count your blessings

In psychological studies of happiness, it turns out that gratitude is a key factor. People who practise gratitude tend to feel better about their lives, are more optimistic about the future, and even sleep better.

In the USA and Canada, one day a year is set aside for giving thanks. Thanksgiving dates back to the 1620s, when the *Mayflower* pilgrims thanked God for a safe journey, a successful settlement, and a good harvest. In fact, so the popular story goes, the Plymouth settlers didn't have those things – but the local Wampanoag people provided food and seed that helped the colony survive.

Today, the festival still serves as a reminder to recognise the abundance in our lives. But don't restrict your gratitude to one day a year. Make giving thanks a regular practice so that it becomes part of your everyday outlook. Start a journal and write down one thing that happened each day for which you're grateful. And don't forget, whenever you have the chance, to simply say, 'Thank you!'

Secret Come to terms with your own mortality
Tradition *Día de Muertos* (Day of the Dead)
Celebrated in Mexico

Dancing with death

Death is a paradox: it is the one certainty in life and the greatest unknown. And for most of us, thoughts of death are unsettling.

One of the most successful rituals for dealing with death is Mexico's *Día de Muertos* fiesta, with origins in pre-Hispanic beliefs that the dead live on in a parallel world and can return to their earthly homes. Ghostly visitors are welcomed with food, flowers and candles, often followed by a visit to the cemetery, where relatives' graves are decorated. Parades of grinning life-sized papier-mâché skeletons are accompanied by mariachi bands, dancing and funfair rides. Shops fill with miniature skulls, coffins and skeletons made of chocolate or marzipan. All this celebration helps Mexican children grow up at ease with the concept of death.

So celebrate your dear departed and take the time to appreciate the days you have left. Accepting that death is part of the bigger picture and not to be feared is the ultimate freedom.

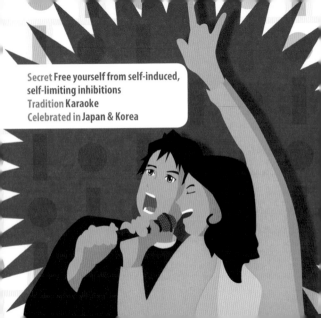

Secret **Free yourself from self-induced, self-limiting inhibitions**
Tradition Karaoke
Celebrated in **Japan & Korea**

Sing your heart out

Most of us aren't naturally gifted singers, but that doesn't mean we can't enjoy belting out a tune. Yet our self-imposed inhibitions can cause us to miss out on a whole host of opportunities.

Karaoke is an excellent study in shedding inhibitions. Do it Japanese style, with friends in a private booth rather than solo at the front of a bar, and it's a team effort to let loose. There is camaraderie to be gained from the shared experience. When everyone has their heart and soul on the line, nobody is a critic. What's more, you'll find that the louder and harder you sing, the more your friends will love you – it opens the door for them to do the same.

Karaoke's enduring popularity all over Japan and Korea testifies to the appeal of socially sanctioned uninhibited behaviour. Even if there's not a karaoke booth nearby, take a note from the playbook and give yourself (and those around you) licence now and then to ditch the self-consciousness.

Secret Keep your mind stimulated
Tradition Saraswati Day (Knowledge Day)
Celebrated in **Bali, Indonesia**

You're never too old to learn new tricks

The brain is a remarkable organ that's incredibly flexible and dynamic. A lack of learning stunts growth and creates boredom, but mental exercise helps ward off cognitive decline in later years.

Balinese Hindus regard our ability to learn as the most important gift for humanity. Paying homage to Saraswati, Hindu goddess of knowledge and learning, they mark their appreciation for learning on Saraswati Day, when children and teachers dress in ceremonial costume. Prayers for increased wisdom are made at schools and in temples, and books are blessed with offerings of flowers and incense.

The tradition reminds us that there are no bounds to our acquisition of knowledge. The great thing is it's so simple to do: read a book, sign up for a course, or take a trip to somewhere new.

A commitment to lifelong learning helps you expand and grow. It gives you the opportunity to stumble upon new interests, develop new skills and uncover innate talents you never even knew you had.

Secret Consider your words before someone takes them to heart
Tradition *Chi Kou* (Day of Dispute)
Celebrated in China

Know when to bite your tongue

If honesty is all that matters, why do words uttered in haste haunt our conscience? We often wonder if we could have struck a better balance between being right and being kind.

The Chinese honour that critical pause between impulse and expression by assigning the third day of the Lunar New Year as the Day of Dispute – a quiet 24 hours when people withdraw from interaction to avoid conflict. On *Chi Kou* (literally, 'red mouth'), all festivities are put on hold. People stay home to regain inner harmony or make their way to temples to pray, then turn in early.

Next time you feel your emotions rising, inhale and count to three, or cast your eyes on the sky to get a sense of the world's immensity. Then, if you still decide to speak, speak slowly, and carefully consider the full impact of your words. You can almost always come up with a gentler and wiser way to phrase your words when you give yourself some time.

Secret Bring your mind back to real time
Tradition *Zazen* (sitting meditation)
Celebrated in Japan

Live in the now

We spend so much time with our heads in the past or the future, we almost forget that our physical selves are forever locked in the present. *Zazen*, which means 'sitting meditation', seeks to bring the body and mind back in line. This practice is the keystone of Zen, a school of Buddhism that emphasises the experiential over creeds.

All you really need to know is how to sit – legs comfortably crossed and with your back straight – and to breathe deeply and mindfully. By concentrating fully on the act of breathing, the mind is naturally drawn to the present. It's harder than you would think, and as anyone who has ever sat through their first 15 minutes of meditation will tell you, time in the present goes a whole lot slower than we realise.

Regular *zazen* meditation can give you a firm footing in the present and even reframe your worldview. And while a quiet corner and a floor cushion would be ideal, we've found that just about anywhere works if you put your mind to it.

Secret Draw on humour and new experiences
to get on with your life
Tradition *Festa del Cornuto* (Festival of Horns)
Celebrated in Rocca Canterano, Italy

Pick yourself up and move on

A bad break-up is traumatic at the best of times, but when you split up because your partner is cheating on you, it can be heartbreaking. You may find yourself asking, 'How can I possibly move on?'

In Rocca Canterano, near Rome, a festival is held in honour of those who had a love-rat partner. Actors parade through the street, recounting satirical stories of love's misadventures. It's a wry, unsentimental take on the foibles of the human heart, with little room for self-pity. Participants wear cuckold's horns atop their heads, and festivalgoers seek each other out to ask if they'd like to *fare le corna* ('make horns' – it probably doesn't need much explanation…).

You, too, may find it useful to acknowledge the bittersweet nature of love. An ironic, philosophical perspective on life's ups and downs can help you move on from a relationship gone sour. Take the first steps to mending your heart with some laughter, a shrug of the shoulders…and maybe some horn making.

Secret Spend some time alone to reconnect with your life's direction
Tradition First Nations vision quest
Celebrated in Canada & USA

Let your 'big self' do the talking

Life's a rush. Sometimes you can find yourself carried along by it all, burdened by expectations and daily obligations. What would it take to get back in touch with the part of yourself that has big plans?

In the First Nations tradition, a vision quest is a vital rite of passage in which you find your life's purpose. Most rituals revolve around a time of physical preparation followed by a period of fasting and isolation, often lasting days. During this time, the quester meditates deeply, calling on spirit guides to reveal to them the necessary direction of their lives.

Time alone is hard to find. To hear what your 'big self' is saying, you might need to get away by yourself for a couple of days. Go camping – or, if you're not the outdoor type, hole up in a B&B. At the very least, take a walk to the top of a hill. Then invite your deepest voices to tell you where you need to go in the next part of your life. The shape of your next few years might be a pleasant surprise.

Secret Rid yourself of physical and mental clutter and get your life back under control
Tradition Preparations for *Chūn Jié* (Spring Festival/Chinese New Year)
Celebrated in China

Get your house in order

There are times when things seem a little too disorganised and untidy for comfort. Chaos and clutter pile up – in your home, at work, or in that space inside your head.

Throughout China and in Chinese communities the world over, the Spring Festival is a time of reunion, renewal and looking optimistically towards the future, starting with cleaning house – literally. Households burst into colour with flowers, fruit and poems inscribed on scrolls. Streets are lit with lanterns and decorations, and people greet each other with messages of peace and prosperity. Starting over can include getting new clothes and a haircut, giving gifts and reconciling differences with those around you.

You can make your own fresh start by revitalising and cleaning out those spaces cluttering up your life. Sweep away that junk at home, at work, in your relationships – it'll give you a renewed sense of clarity and purpose, and might even bring on good luck…

Secret Acknowledge your influences
Tradition Visiting teachers
Celebrated in Vietnam

Recognise your teachers

Despite the horrors that school can inflict, you can usually remember at least one teacher who took some kind of interest in you. They taught you something that went beyond the textbook, and maybe it pointed you in a career direction. Maybe it just made you feel a little better about yourself, or a little smarter.

In Vietnam's lunar new year celebration, days one and two are reserved for family and friends. But day three? Visiting your teachers! Teachers are highly respected in Vietnamese society. People take time to acknowledge their presence in their lives (past or present), and to thank them, especially on this day, with gifts.

It might not be so easy to visit a teacher from your distant past. So, a project: acknowledge the impact of a teacher in your life. Write about them. Jot down the important things they said to you. What was happening in your life at the time? What would you say to them if you could? You may find some insight into the path you're on.

Secret Accept that you aren't always in control and have faith
Tradition Prayer
Celebrated Around the world

Faith can move mountains

We all need to feel a sense of control over our lives. Yet there is so much that we can't control. Faith allows us to put all those worries on the table and accept things the way they are. What will be, will be.

In cultures all over the world, faith is rooted in religion. Counting rosary beads in Italy, bowing to Mecca in Saudi Arabia, inserting notes into the Western Wall in Jerusalem – through the medium of prayer, believers offer up their concerns in an act of surrender.

Having faith doesn't have to mean praying to an external, interventionist being. Faith in humanistic values allows us to get on a plane and trust the skill of the pilot. It allows us to put our money in banks, undergo an operation, or climb a mountain.

Let go of the things that are out of your hands, and work on aspects of your life that you can control. Try saying a few words to God, whatever that means to you – to your guardian angel, your guru, or just the world in general – and feel the weight lift off your shoulders.

BODY

Secret Exercise to produce endorphins, and get a physical and mental workout
Tradition T'ai chi
Celebrated in Shanghai, China

Stretch your body and mind

You probably shouldn't have eaten that last slice of pizza. Or that half tub of choc-chip. Lying in bed till noon is only adding to your sense of bloat and torpor. When your body's in bad condition, your mind similarly festers; but conversely, the buzz from increased physical fitness gives the brain a boost.

Head to Shanghai's Bund to see this mind-body rejuvenation in slo-mo action. Every day at dawn, the waterfront flexes with locals practising t'ai chi: old and young performing an ancient martial art. Some wave swords; others stand in a state of utter tranquillity. It's a slow, balletic display: a meditation in motion.

Try t'ai chi yourself – all ages can manage its subtle movements, and any practice space will do (though rising at dawn and heading outside may bring even greater mental clarity). If you don't fancy learning a martial art, find another sport you enjoy to get the blood pumping, the body toning and – as a result – the mind on a high.

Secret Take the time to appreciate
good food and drink
Tradition Ethiopian Buna
(Coffee) Ceremony
Celebrated in Ethiopia

The finer things in life

When did you last take the time to really savour the food you eat? We grab takeaway meals and coffee, but dining 'on the run' represents a missed opportunity for enjoyment on many levels.

A slower pace of life is exemplified in the Ethiopian Coffee Ceremony, a 3000-year-old ritual that stimulates all the senses. It is performed by a woman wearing a traditional white dress, who carefully arranges the coffee-making implements on top of ceremonial grasses while incense burns. Green coffee beans are washed and roasted until they pop and change colour. The host grinds them, brews the coffee and pours it from a long-spouted *jebena*. Etiquette requires guests to consume three cupfuls of the coffee: the third cup, the *baraka*, invokes a blessing.

Life is too short for bad coffee and bland convenience foods. Food and drink are one of life's simple but remarkable pleasures, so choose your favourites, slow down…and enjoy.

Secret **Take some time out to recharge your batteries**
Tradition *Shabbat* (Sabbath)
Celebrated in **Israel**

And on the seventh day...

It's easy to slip into a pattern where every moment of your time is assigned to busyness and it's hard to take any time out. Rushing between job and home, trying to fulfil obligations: when do you stop to watch a bird fly across the sky or feel your own heartbeat?

The Jewish tradition of *Shabbat* sanctifies a day of rest in imitation of the divine – for after creating the world, God rested for a day. Orthodox Jews observe strict *Shabbat* laws that forbid such actions as turning on lights and driving cars. The day is often spent with the family, eating special meals; a nap is not uncommon. Despite the prohibitions, *Shabbat* is eagerly awaited and welcomed with feast foods, special clothes and spruced houses.

What would happen if you instituted the practice of reserving a day of absolute rest for yourself? It doesn't have to be every week but it's surprisingly refreshing to allow yourself a day of blissful nothing. You might find it becomes your favourite routine!

Secret **Learn to be comfortable with your body**
Tradition **Naked saunas**
Celebrated in **Finland**

Shed your skin

Whose dumb idea was it to be ashamed of our bodies? Most people have at least a slight case of physical unease when seeing themselves naked; and yet our bodies are our finest instruments of awareness and connection. They are…ourselves. Isn't it time they got a little respect?

Feeling comfortable with nudity is built into the culture in Scandinavian Europe. Finland, in particular, is renowned for its communal saunas, followed by icy splash downs, followed by more saunas…and all without a stitch on. The young, the old, the willowy, the wobbly – everyone's into the idea of a building up a healthy and invigorating sweat, and never mind the shyness.

Your culture may not be of the let-it-all-hang-out variety, but think of all the great experiences your body has been central to (your first kiss, learning to play the piano, eating that crème brûlée in Paris). Stand in front of a mirror and see the beauty that is particularly your own. You'll be well on your way to your first skinny-dip.

Secret Realise your connection to the natural world

Tradition Summer solstice at Glastonbury Tor

Celebrated in Glastonbury, England

Let nature
make your heart sing

We may believe we're makers of our own destiny, but occasionally the irresistible power of mother nature takes over. Everyone's mood declines in winter only to uplift on a sunny day; the urge to clean grips us in spring; and other urges surface in summer. If we slow down and breathe deep, we can all feel the rhythms of nature ebb and flow within us, no matter how little we know of its mysteries.

For millennia, pagans on every continent celebrated seasonal transitions as the summer and winter solstices, the longest and shortest days of the year. Postmodern English Druids camp out at ancient sites like Glastonbury Tor to await the sunrise on the summer solstice and listen to the call of nature carried on the wings of sunbeams as they stretch across the verdant valley.

It is the song we hold in our hearts even as we wander the city and stay up watching late-night TV. It is the music that will lift your spirit and set you free.

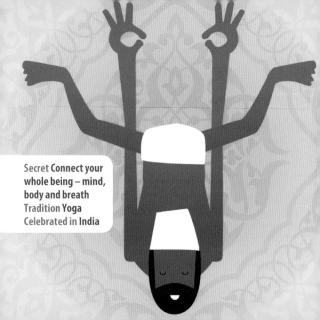

Secret **Connect your whole being – mind, body and breath**
Tradition **Yoga**
Celebrated in **India**

Don't forget to breathe

Our minds are inherently connected to our bodies; stress brings on sweating and tense muscles, fear makes us shiver. But the converse is also true: we can use our body to alter our mind for the better.

A core concept of the ancient Indian practice of yoga is the connection of mind and body through the function of the breath. Concentrating on breathing keeps the mind focused on the body.

Deep, steady breathing encourages physical relaxation: blood pressure is lowered, and resources that might be held ready for 'fight or flight' responses are allocated to healing other bodily systems. As the body recharges, the mind is stilled, leading to a sense of peace.

Using your breath to control mind and body can be a powerful technique in times of pain or stress, as any midwife can attest. Next time you find yourself strapped in a dentist's chair, running late for a meeting or in any situation that has you reaching for the headache pills, remember to stop, calm your thoughts, and *breathe*.

Secret Talk to your neighbours to reconnect with your community
Tradition *La passeggiata*
Celebrated in Italy

Break out of your bubble

Maybe it's the gadgets, maybe it's your work life, but it's easy to get lost in your own private universe and end up isolated and alone.

The perfect antidote to a feeling of isolation is *la passeggiata*, or evening stroll, an age-old ritual in Italy. It's a fail-safe way to ensure those face-to-face meetings that create true community.

As late afternoon passes into early evening, Italians throng the pavements and squares, walking, talking, sharing a drink or gelato. Whether it's about socialising with old friends, flirting with new or just people-watching, the *passeggiata* reminds you that you're part of something bigger, that your community is there for you.

Taking a stroll with other people can pick up your spirits – both the exercise and the camaraderie play a part. But anything that gets you out in your community can do the trick. Volunteer, reach out to a neighbour, think about one aspect of your life that could be made more social – these things remind you that you're not alone.

Secret **Face your fears to overcome them**
Tradition **N'gol (land diving)**
Celebrated in **Pentecost Island, Vanuatu**

Fear less, be more

Whether you're next in line to skydive, or you have to speak at a conference, none of us are strangers to fear. Succumb to fear, and you're screwed: the only solution is to face our fears.

On Pentecost Island in Vanuatu, the locals have a tradition that's basically bungee jumping but using vines. The N'gol ritual involves stripping a tall tree and building a platform to jump off near the summit. Ironically, only males get to make the leap of faith.

It's ironic because as well as being a fertility ritual, N'gol honours the legend of a woman who hid in a tree from her violent husband, and tied liana vines to her feet before leaping from his clutches as he climbed up to kill her. Not realising the vines had broken her fall, her husband too made the jump…to his death.

Whatever you fear, climb your N'gol ladder, stare into the eyes of what terrifies you most, and launch yourself 30m down onto the mud. What's the worst that can happen?

Secret Allow yourself to luxuriate
**Tradition Steaming and scrubbing
in a hammam**
Celebrated in **Turkey**

Ready, set, pamper!

When was the last time you took the time to really relax, feeling it right down to your bones? When it comes to kicking back, not many countries beat Turkey, with its centuries-old tradition of bathing – preferably in 17th-century marble hammams. Lolling around on warmed stone, sweating luxuriously, dousing yourself with cool water, summoning an attendant to rub you down – can't you just feel your worries dissolving with the steam?

What, there's no bathhouse in your home town? Splurging on the occasional massage (or, better still, swapping one with your nearest and dearest) is a delightful way to relax. Make sure there are plenty of fragrant oils involved. If you want that genuine steamy feel, run yourself a warm bath and lounge around in the scented water until your fingertips go soft. Or if that's out of your reach, pick a sunny day and lie on the floweriest, deepest grass you can find, letting the warmth sink right down into you. See? That's relaxed.

Secret Make some silent time
to allow your head to clear
Tradition Nyepi (Day of Silence)
Celebrated in **Bali, Indonesia**

Turn down the volume

Life is a cacophony: people talking, phones ringing, children whining, advertisements blaring. Exposure to a constant din has been shown to increase blood pressure, and the babble makes it hard to hear yourself think, to take stock and sort out your priorities.

The Balinese set aside the first day of the new year for silence and contemplation, to purify and allow for new beginnings. When *Nyepi* dawns, all activity ceases. No-one works, no vehicles may be used, no electric appliances are operated, and everyone must stay off the streets. The story goes that evil spirits will be fooled into thinking that Bali has been abandoned and will leave the island unharmed for another year. But it's also a time to meditate and reflect, to liberate the mind from worldly distractions, and emerge refreshed.

Find a private place to spend a few hours in peace and quiet – no activity, no telephone, no TV. You may find that the demons running around your head get so bored, they leave you alone.

Secret **Get outside whenever possible**
Tradition Midsummer Festival
Celebrated in Sweden

A little sunshine
can go a long way

Being cooped up indoors gets you lethargic and listless; a certain amount of fresh air and light are essential to our well-being. We need those sunrays to produce vitamin D for our health.

The Swedes take to the outdoors with great merriment to celebrate the the longest day of the year at the Midsummer Festival. With origins in early religious and fertility rites, the modern festival is a time to rejoice in the light and natural beauty of summertime. Families flock to the countryside to eat, drink, dance and sing around maypoles decorated with fresh flowers and greenery. According to folklore, elements of nature have special, even magical powers during Midsummer's Eve.

A little fresh air and sunlight can work like magic for you, too. You don't have to wait for summer: just slop on some sunscreen and treat yourself to the mood-boosting effects of fresh air and sun-induced vitamin D on a regular basis. Hello sunshine!

Secret **Express yourself physically**
Tradition *Céilí* dancing
Celebrated in **Ireland**

Let your body do the talking

For many of us, much of our daily routine consists of sitting at a desk, jostling for space on trains or getting stuck in traffic. Inactivity inevitably leads to headaches, backache and stress.

Dancing releases tension, boosts confidence and improves well-being. An Irish *céilí* is social dancing at its most community minded, a raucous celebration of life where the most important thing is joining in. No-one will glare when you step on their toes; you'll just be dragged along in the right direction, spun faster and encouraged with a great big smile. *Céilídh* are all about the *craic* (fun), and it's hard to feel stressed when you're twirling around a room so fast you're afraid what might happen if your partner lets go.

Céilí is just one way of strutting your stuff. You can turn up the music and prance around your bedroom in your undies, hit your local nightclub, join a salsa class, sway, slide, wriggle or rock. It doesn't have to cost a thing, and is guaranteed to make you smile.

Secret Go without to appreciate what you have
Tradition Ramadan
Celebrated in Egypt

Discipline is not a dirty word

When we're bombarded with pleas to buy the hottest gadgets, must-have new toys and best-value meal combos, it's easy to fall prey to overindulgence and excessive consumption.

For a month every year, Muslims in Egypt and across the world turn the tables on the pursuit of more and instead go without. From dawn to dusk during the holy month of Ramadan, not a morsel of food or a drop of water will pass the lips of Egyptian Muslims as a reminder of how lucky they are to possess what they have. It's a time of deep reflection on the blessings of life, where all become equal. Ramadan evenings are especially joyous, as people gather to enjoy the simple pleasures of drinking and eating after the day of fasting.

You don't need to be a Muslim to carry out a fast. But if it seems too extreme, why not deny yourself that extra coffee or muffin for a month, and put the money towards a favourite good cause. You'll find yourself smiling at the multitude of blessings you actually have.

Secret Dress yourself up to create beauty where you see none
Tradition Dressing up, Soninke style
Celebrated in Mali, Niger & eastern Senegal

You are what you wear

When your world, or just your day, falls apart, it can be easy to fall apart with it. But when things look sad, take a step back. There's room for beauty, too, and if you can't find it, you can always create it.

In the Sahel region of Africa, nomadic groups such as the Soninke spend their days traversing a landscape of scrubland and sun-seared desert, their belongings piled high on donkeys. In the dry season, the heat is scalding. In the wet, it's suffocating.

But how pretty they look! Gold hoops are laced through ears. Dresses are long and red. Hair is braided and eyes are lined with bright blue. Juxtaposed against the lonely landscapes, the women in particular can show us a thing or two about beauty.

When you feel lost in no-man's land, raid your jewellery box and throw on a pair of sparkles, go shopping in the back of your own closet or dig out that red lipstick. Don't fade into your surroundings. That tough place you're in right now? It's not you. It's just a place.

Secret Get things off your chest with like-minded others
Tradition *Stammtisch* (regulars' table)
Celebrated in **Germany**

Talk about it

You think football is the greatest. Or you've just had a baby and it's changed your entire life. But sometimes the people around you don't share your interests, or find your enthusiasm a little weird.

In Germany, friends, colleagues and interested strangers get together regularly at *Stammtisches* to chat, laugh, spark connections and get a fresh perspective on subjects that interest them. Once only open to the town's elite, who would share news over drinks at the local restaurant or pub, *Stammtisches* have become a way for people with common passions or hobbies to meet up. Groups have formed around every subject imaginable, and the people you meet at *Stammtisch* groups seldom stay strangers for long.

Why not book a table somewhere and give a few like-minded friends a call? Ask them to invite friends of their own, put some posters up around town, spread the word online, and before long, the conversation will be flowing as fast as the beer.

Secret Discover what's deep inside with
a physical challenge
Tradition Self-transcendence marathon
Celebrated in **Queens, New York City, USA**

Test your limits to transcend your self

Maybe you run, or work out in the gym. You know a good session clears your mind. But what about taking on something so physically and mentally difficult, you don't know whether you'll be capable?

Each summer, a block in Queens becomes the backdrop for the 4988km (3100-mile) Self-Transcendence Marathon – the longest footrace in the world. Runners complete the equivalent of two full marathons (84km/52 miles) each day to cover the distance within the 52-day limit. Founded by spiritual teacher Sri Chinmoy, who prescribed extraordinary physical and mental feats to expand the mind, the race is the ultimate test of survival and endurance, in which participants must truly transcend themselves.

The spirit of this challenge is to gain self-knowledge by achieving something that's difficult, *for you*. Whatever your goal, realising it will give you a new certainty that you can find a strength deep within yourself and overcome your own perceived limits.

SPIRIT

Secret **Shut down business as usual and go a bit wild**
Tradition **Carnaval**
Celebrated in **Brazil**

Let Loose

In a world that's open for business 24/7, it's easy to feel like a dutiful drudge. But what if there was an entire week when your culture asked you to drop everything and simply celebrate being alive?

Brazil's annual Carnaval is just such a party. Business as usual is shut down, the social order is flipped on its head, and everybody is reminded that the things that matter in life can't be measured on spreadsheets. Blending African beats, Native American-inspired costumes and Bacchanalian traditions with roots in ancient Europe, Carnaval is a celebration of diversity and creative self-expression, an exuberant, nonstop frenzy of music, dancing and sensuality.

Even if you can't make it to Brazil, you can join carnival festivities closer to home. Or why not get together with friends and plot your own creative release? Find a way to let go of the status quo for a few days every year. Without a doubt, these are the times you'll remember on your deathbed, not your regular nine to five.

"HA HA HA ho ho HO ho ho ho HO ho HO ho ho HO ho HA HA HO HA ho HA ho"

Secret Take life less seriously
Tradition Hasya yoga
(laughter therapy)
Celebrated in India

Laugh it off

A scowl from a colleague, a snide remark, the discovery of another grey hair...whatever the cause, we are masters of dwelling on negative thoughts, allowing them to mess with our minds.

Starting with chants of 'Ho Ho Ha Ha' and culminating in deep belly guffaws, the Indian practice of Hasya yoga or laughter therapy recognises the health benefits of laughter. They apply whether or not the laughter is genuine, and therein lies the medicinal magic.

Reports indicate that adults laugh, on average, only 15 times a day compared to the childhood average of 350. Yet laughter has been scientifically proven to significantly enhance overall well-being: it relaxes muscles, triggers the release of 'happy' hormones, clears respiratory passages and radically elevates mood.

Make it a point to greet each day with a jolly good chuckle. Stretch your arms in the air, close your eyes, take some deep breaths, then Ho Ho Ha Ha your way to a happier, healthier you.

Secret Realise your connection to place
Tradition Garma Festival
Celebrated in Gulkula, northeast
Arnhem Land, Australia

Home is where the earth is

When we feel out of time and out of place, it's good to remember the fixed points in life: things that remain constant, like memories or notions of home and that sense of place that calls to us.

Each August the Yolngu people come together to reconnect to place during the Garma Festival, held in a stringybark forest where the ancestral didgeridoo was brought to the Yolngu. It's a land criss-crossed by traditional songlines, those tracks and sites where ancestor beings called the country into existence. The connection with country is tangible in the shades of ochre on skin, the feel and taste of the dust kicked up from dancers' feet, the sound of the didgeridoo and smell of the stringybarks.

Connections can be made anywhere; it's partly about paying attention. See that tree in the garden or park? Watch it over time. Notice its – and your – response as seasons pass. And, as the world moves on, begin to feel more connected; more at home.

Secret **Wash away the old and welcome the new**
Tradition **Songkran (Thai New Year)**
Celebrated in **Thailand**

Spring-clean mind, body and spirit

Time slips away like water. One minute we're making New Year's resolutions, the next we're wondering where the year went. If only we could wipe the slate clean and start afresh.

Songkran, or Thai New Year, celebrates the sun moving into Aries with the ultimate spring-clean of mind, body and spirit. Thais send water balloons and buckets flying, aim water pistols at passing motorcyclists and túk-túks, and even bring in the odd elephant to drench the crowds. *Songkran* is a time of new beginnings, when Thais scrub their homes and clean Buddha images, washing away last year's dirt and, hopefully, sins and bad luck too. It's a time for paying respects to elderly relatives and giving alms to monks.

You can bring a little *Songkran* into your life any time. Clean your house, resolve to leave any unpleasantness from the past behind, and look forward to a bright future. Through positive thinking we can achieve clarity and peace of mind, and let the good karma flow.

Secret **Spend time with family to understand your context**
Tradition **Tsagaan Sar (White Month)**
Celebrated in **Mongolia**

Respect your elders

Leaving home can make us forget our commitment to family and the role we play in it. At risk is our past: our traditions and the lessons taught to us by our elders.

Mongolian New Year is a time for families to honour the elder members of the clan. They are greeted with a clasping of the arms known as a *zolgokh*. This gesture includes the passing of a blue or white silk scarf, representing the clear sky and purity of the soul. Children and grandchildren utter words of respect for their elders, recalling their wisdom, compassion and generosity.

A calendar is hardly necessary for carrying out these Mongol rites. Make it a weekly or a monthly practice to reconnect with the elder members of your family. Call if you're far from home or visit if you're nearby.

Spending time to reconnect gives you a sense of place and a better understanding of how and where you fit in with your mob.

Secret Embrace the painful past with a light heart
Tradition *Festival de Diablos y Congos* (Festival of the Devils and Congos)
Celebrated in Portobelo, Panamá

Turn the tables on history

Remembering displacement, enslavement and injustice make us uneasy, but it's important: when ancestors' stories are lost, so is a culture's sense of identity. It takes courage to reckon with the past – and even more to play with it.

In Portobelo, the Devils and Congos Festival celebrates slaves who fled their Spanish colonial masters for the rainforest. Their descendants, known as Congos, travel the crowd 'kidnapping' spectators for outrageous ransoms (a few coins can purchase your release). Their colourful rags mock the finery of the Spanish and their reverse speech emulates ancestors who spoke mutiny in codes.

Congo art also reclaims identity; self-portraits are often framed by mirror shards, which both admit damage and pick up the pieces.

These expressions show how to honour the past by reclaiming even its thorny parts. With a light heart, it's possible to revisit hardship. Parody your enemies, but make peace too.

Secret Refresh your perspective and seek the good in life
Tradition *Diwali or Deepavali* **(Festival of Lights)**
Celebrated in India

Illuminate your spirit

Through life's hardships and challenges, sometimes we need to recalibrate, sweep clean and start anew. Circumstances change, but creating an environment of positivity can be a constant.

In India, *Diwali* provides just this opportunity to embrace peace over pain, in life and within your spirit, and start fresh. During the Hindu celebration, people cleanse and prepare to welcome Lakshmi, the Goddess of Good Fortune, as well as gods like Hanuman and Ganesha – the Remover of Obstacles and Lord of Auspicious Beginnings. Houses and shops are swept and whitewashed and skies are ablaze with fireworks. Glittering rows of single-wick lamps line rooftops and window sills.

Bring the spirit of *Diwali* into your daily life. Clean a room from top to bottom. Feeling ambitious? Pick a wall and paint it a fresh, hopeful colour. Light candles, warm your own heart, and share some loving hopefulness and anticipation with someone else.

Secret **Embrace your heritage**
to better understand yourself
Tradition **Maori haka**
Celebrated in **New Zealand**

Be proud of your roots

The world is homogenising: many people no longer feel part of something, and instead we feel lonely and lacking in identity. But reconnecting with our heritage can confer a greater sense of self.

Take the Maori. A *haka* is a traditional form of dance, with many variants – some are war cries, some are welcomes, while others are ceremonial displays. Despite its fearsome fist-waving and tongue-poking, 'Kamate Kamate' – the New Zealand All Blacks' iconic prematch spine-tingler – is not a call to arms on the rugby pitch. It celebrates a past chief's evasion of the army sent to kill him, yet this ritual now stands for much more. It unites Kiwis of all backgrounds, and it scares the bejesus out of the opposition…

So find your own *haka*. Ask relatives about their past, or research your family tree. Don't be afraid to cheer for your 'team' (village, ethnic group, nation). This isn't about nationalism at its flag-waving worst. It's a celebration that helps you feel kinship with your clan.

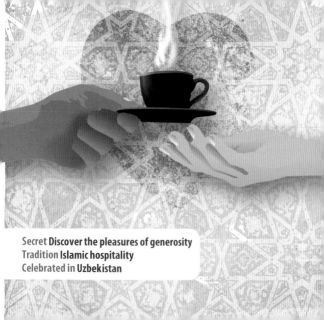

Secret Discover the pleasures of generosity
Tradition Islamic hospitality
Celebrated in Uzbekistan

Kindness to strangers

Children are taught that strangers are dangerous. Adults lock car doors at traffic lights and secure their houses. Yes, the world can be hostile, but a culture of fear robs us of the pleasure of giving help and open welcome to a fellow human being.

In areas of Central Asia, particularly rural ones, it's customary to give everything to the guest, even if it's all you have – and even if the guest is a stranger. In Uzbekistan, a host would traditionally slaughter a sheep to feed a stranger, offering them the choicest delicacies from the animal's head.

There are plenty of ways to extend the hand of selfless friendship to someone you've never met before. That tourist struggling with tickets, map and an unfamiliar language? Offer them help. That new guy in your office? Invite him to lunch with your friendliest colleagues. Or maybe just give the coat off your back to a charity this winter. It's guaranteed to warm the cockles of your heart!

Secret Recognise and celebrate your accomplishments
Tradition Crop Over
Celebrated in Barbados, Lesser Antilles

Savour the fruits of your labour

With our time-poor lifestyles, any sense of achievement is crushed under the daily grind, and it's easy to forget what our hard work is for.

The Crop Over festival in Barbados encompasses entertainment and heritage events including calypso music, food and drink, parades and partying. Festivities culminate in the Grand Kadooment, a procession of costumed revellers dancing through the streets.

The festival's origins date back to the 1780s, when plantation workers celebrated the end of the sugar-cane harvest. They held a procession of carts bringing in the last loads of the crop, followed by a time of rejoicing for the completion of all their hard work; an occasion to celebrate and enjoy the fruits of one's labour.

It's good to step back every now and then to acknowledge what you've accomplished. Those tasks can wait a little while longer, and it'll be good for your sense of purpose and self-worth to reflect on how far you've come. Go on –you've earned it.

Secret **Find the ultimate contentment in friends, family and a good book**
Tradition *Hygge* ('cosiness')
Celebrated in **Denmark**

Get back to basics

The greatest contentment in life can come from simplification, from paring pleasures down to their most basic. The Danes are well aware of this, which is probably why they continually top global happiness surveys. And it's much to do with their concept of *hygge*.

Pronounced 'whoo-ger', it defies direct translation, but evokes a sense of cosiness and inner warmth – like sharing a nice bottle of red around an open fire. It's songs around the tree at Christmas and sausages on the grill in summer. No stress, no complications – just comfort and a sense of being completely at ease with the world.

Hygge is easy to find – you just need to make the time for it. Organise a few days away, off-grid: it doesn't have to be expensive, just gather some friends and find a campsite. Turn off the computer and swap virtual friends for real ones – invite them over for a cuppa and a chat. Or simply curl up on the sofa with a blanket and a good book. There, you're in *hygge* heaven.

Celebrate the dirty work

We are living in the age of the individual. We learn to meet our own needs, and just as we never want to ask for help, sometimes we may be slow to give it. But it behoves us to recognise that collaboration can be as viable a survival skill as self-sufficiency.

On the Chilean archipelago of Chiloe, the *minga* is an event where neighbours offer up their sweat and toil for the feast that follows. The tradition is rooted in the history of fishermen and subsistence farmers who have always had to rely on each other for hard physical labour. It can mean harvesting potatos, shingling a barn or hitching up teams of oxen to put a whole house on logs and then roll it to a new location. In thanks, the host barbecues a whole lamb or gathers up a seafood feast.

What if we brought collective survival into our own lives? Offer yourself up for dirty work. When you're in need, ask for help with the hard stuff, then reward your friends with a celebration.

Secret Enjoy life now because
you never know what's ahead
Tradition Mardi Gras (Fat Tuesday)
Celebrated in New Orleans, USA

Carpe diem

From an early age we're told what we *should* and *shouldn't* do. The rules, the fear of what others think, can end up governing our lives.

But a few days on the calendar allow everyone, young and old, to live in the *now*, and New Orleans has one of the best: Mardi Gras. It is a day when we all can wear face paint and skip in the streets as if we were children released from the should-shouldn't prison.

Mardi Gras is the culmination of the Carnival season, the last day before the start of Lenten restrictions, and is often viewed as a day of excess, with liquor and mayhem figuring prominently.

Outside of Mardi Gras, commit to doing one thing each day that makes it your own. You may not feel like wearing a feather boa and rumba-ing down the hall to the water cooler at work, but you could hold a gyrating boogie session in your living room. Wear a bright stripy scarf. Or simply take time out to gaze at the night sky.

The past is gone and the future is uncertain – so seize today!

Secret Appreciate the Gift of Family
Tradition *Raksha Bandhan*
Celebrated in India

The ties that bind

Your family may be a collection of clashing personalities, but they are some of the closest ties you'll have in life. Who else can say they really knew you way back when?

Hindus in India celebrate the brother–sister bond in a festival known as *Raksha Bandhan,* 'the bond of protection'. Girls say prayers for their brothers, prepare special foods and ceremoniously tie a *rakhi,* or bracelet, made of cotton or silk on each brother's right wrist. This symbolises affection, love and protection from harm.

In turn, girls are lavished with gifts from their brothers, who bless them and promise to look out for them in the year ahead. Cousins, aunts and uncles can be honoured too.

Is there something special you can do for someone in your family, a way to celebrate and strengthen your unique bond? While friends come and go, family will always be connected to us. They can provide a safe haven and are the source of some of life's most joyful moments.

Secret **Give away something you value to appreciate how lucky you are**
Tradition *Inati* (sharing)
Celebrated in **The Pacific Islands, especially Tokelau & Cook Islands**

Share your bounty

Many of us scarcely know our neighbours, let alone consider their well-being. We're all focused on our own progress and needs, making sure 'I'm all right Jack'.

On tiny Tokelau, such individualism isn't an option. Comprising three low-lying coral atolls – a 20-hour boat ride from nearest neighbour, Samoa – remote Tokelau can only function if its tiny population works together. Those who have help those who have not by practising the system of *inati* (sharing). Every day, the fresh catch is laid out on the beach and the village *taupulega* (council) dishes it out according to who needs it most.

Embrace the principles of *inati* in your community. Could you make meals for an elderly neighbour? Or give away the spoils of your veggie patch to friends without gardens? Perhaps it's skills and time you could share. Offer to fix a fence or help with a tax return, and realise how fortunate you are to be in the position to offer some help.

Secret Moderate your life and be flexible
Tradition *Obangsaek* (traditional five
colours in harmony)
Celebrated in Korea

In all things, balance

While personal-growth gurus preach self-care, seeking harmony through balance has long been an Eastern tradition.

In Korea, the *obangsaek* (traditional five colours) of red, black, yellow, white and green/blue correspond to the elements and to our five basic tastes: bitter, salty, sweet, spicy and sour. By balancing these components in one dish and creating harmony in colour and taste, you draw power and promote health and happiness.

The principle is illustrated by the quintessential Korean meal *bibimbap*, in which equal quantities of julienned ingredients such as carrot, dark pyogo mushroom, white bellflower root and green water parsley are laid around a yellow egg yolk on a bowl of rice. It's in the mixing before eating that the whole becomes greater than the parts.

It's worth considering which elements of your life are out of balance. Take a lesson from this colourful cuisine: mixing it up more equally can be a beautiful thing.

Secret **Release your inner child and play**
Tradition **Holi**
Celebrated in **India**

Colour up your life

We strive for jobs, material goods, better relationships. In the heart-racing strive-athon of life, our in-a-hurry inner adult can asphyxiate our inner child, leaving us frazzled and disenchanted.

Feeling strived out? Hello Holi! This Hindu Festival of Colours sees people jump off the treadmill of life to unleash their inner child as merrymakers playfully douse one another with water and fistfuls of coloured powder to celebrate the onset of spring. It's a time for indulging in delicious *mithai* (Indian sweets) and special *lassi* drink laced with almonds, pistachios or rose petals. Bonfires are lit to symbolise the demise of Holika, a wicked demoness.

Why not colour your life up, Holi style? A water-fight in the backyard followed by feasting with friends will wash away pent-up stress. Or symbolically burn your personal demons by jotting down your worries on scraps of paper, sending them into the fireplace and watching them disappear in (Holi) smoke.

Secret Realise your interconnectedness with others
Tradition The philosophy of *ubuntu*
Celebrated in **South Africa**

How to be human

The cult of the individual is paramount in the West, but the distinctly African concept of *ubuntu* is the understanding that no human exists in isolation. Translated as 'I am only a person through other people', it recognises that everything one does affects others, and that the welfare of each is dependent upon the welfare of all.

This means that Africans will invite strangers into their homes and feed them when they are hungry. It means children are raised with the input of a village rather than letting parents struggle on their own. Because interdependence works both ways, it means people are willing to accept help, as well as give it. This philosophy is celebrated in the Ubuntu Festival held every July in Cape Town.

Practising *ubuntu* can be as simple as cultivating empathy. Listen to others, and put yourself in their shoes. Volunteering your time with a charity is a great way to find that sense of belonging and unity. And if you need help, ask for it – you don't have to do it all alone!

INDEX

ACKNOWLEDGEMENTS

PUBLISHER
Piers Pickard

COMMISSIONING EDITOR
Jessica Cole

EDITOR
Kate James

DESIGNER
Marika Mercer

DESIGN DELIVERY MANAGER
Brendan Dempsey

THANKS
Larissa Frost

WRITTEN BY
Alexis Averbuck (p103, 115), Sarah Baxter (p15, 25, 29, 57, 105, 111, 119), Bridget Blair (p13, 33, 35, 53, 67, 75, 125), Piera Chen (p41), Nigel Chin (p45, 49, 109), Kerry Christiani (p97), Gregor Clark (p69, 91), Lisa Dunford (p121), Ben Handicott (p17, 51), Virginia Jealous (p95), Michael Kohn (p99), Jessica Lee (p81), Alex Leviton (introduction), Emily Matchar (p19), Carolyn McCarthy (p101, 113), Rebecca Milner (p37, 43), Gabi Mocatta (p87), Rose Mulready (p21, 23, 27, 47, 61, 63, 73, 107), Etain O'Carroll (p79), Dan Savery Raz (p31), Craig Scutt (p65, 71), Sarina Singh (p93, 123), Meredith Snyder (p85), Kate Thomas (p83), Caroline Veldhuis (p39, 59, 77, 117)

ILLUSTRATED BY
Mark Adams (p12, 46, 86, 108), Peter Caddy (p40, 90, 122), Samantha Curcio (p20, 30, 68, 84, 92), Hugh Ford (p18, 36, 50, 58, 66, 76, 82, 100, 116), Andy Lewis (p14, 26, 42, 56, 78, 96, 102, 110, 118), Christopher Ong (p16, 32, 48, 60, 74, 80, 104), Michael Ruff (p22, 38, 44, 52, 94, 98, 106, 112, 124)

COVER DESIGN BY
Mark Adams and Dan Baird

PICTURE CREDITS
Age Fotostock (p116), Getty Images (p14, 16, 20, 24, 28, 34, 46, 64, 68, 70, 72, 86, 94, 114, 120, 124), iStock (p92), Lonely Planet (p62)

LONELY PLANET OFFICES

Australia – Locked Bag 1, Footscray,
Victoria 3011
Ph 03 8379 8000 **Fax** 03 8379 8111
Email talk2us@lonelyplanet.com.au

USA – 150 Linden St, Oakland, CA 94607
Ph 510 250 6400 **Toll Free** 800 275 8555
Fax 510 893 8572
Email info@lonelyplanet.com

UK – Media Centre, 201 Wood Lane,
London W12 7TQ
Ph 020 8433 1333 **Fax** 020 8702 0112
Email go@lonelyplanet.co.uk

HAPPY
March 2015

PUBLISHED BY
Lonely Planet Publications Pty Ltd
ABN 36 005 607 983
lonelyplanet.com

ISBN 978-1-74360-760-2
Text © Lonely Planet 2015
Photos & illustrations © as indicated 2015
Printed in China
10 9 8 7 6 5 4 3 2 1

MIX
Paper from
responsible sources
FSC™ C021741
www.fsc.org

Paper in this book is certified against
the Forest Stewardship Council™ standards.
FSC™ promotes environmentally responsible,
socially beneficial and economically viable
management of the world's forests.